# POCAHONTAS
## PRINCESS OF THE NEW WORLD

### KATHLEEN KRULL

### PICTURES BY DAVID DIAZ

WALKER & COMPANY 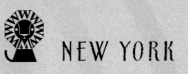 NEW YORK

Even at eleven years old, Pocahontas was quite the royal princess. She was kind and compassionate, of course, and clever and fearless. She had the proper doting father. Everyone around gave her the proper respect. And she knew how to get her own way—as a proper princess must.

The year was 1607, a sunny day in May. Leaves in all shades of green flickered in the breeze. On such a heavenly day, a girl who was a princess might be dancing, not working.

The place was the lush Chesapeake Bay, in what is now Virginia. Thousands of Powhatan Indians thrived here, in a forest so dense it was more like a jungle. One of them was this dancing girl—Matoaka, known by her nickname: Pocahontas.

She was the daughter of the fiercest warrior of eastern Virginia. From his royal lodge, Chief Powhatan ruled over thirty tribes. We don't know her mother's name. The chief had many wives.

As a baby, Pocahontas had been washed in cold water every morning, to toughen her up. Now her long legs were powerful, from sprinting through the forest. So were her arms, from paddling her dugout canoe. Marriage—and less freedom—would be coming soon enough. For now she was a girl in motion, asking questions, laughing and teasing, getting attention.

And always she danced in the moonlight. Powhatan Indians knew this dense forest by heart—all the plants, all the animals, and especially all the dangers. They worked so hard each day that they had time for music and dancing almost every night.

In the Powhatan world, women—not just Pocahontas—had high status. Women were the farmers, harvesting corn, squash, beans, and the sacred herb, tobacco. They also built the houses, which were cool and mosquito-free in the summers, toasty in the winters.

Princess Pocahontas probably avoided certain jobs. She couldn't be seen burying garbage. Perhaps she helped to make pottery, stitch beadwork, or weave baskets. Or perhaps she just cartwheeled and joked her way out of chores.

Now, on this breezy day in May, Pocahontas whirled on, unaware of the danger. Three ships loomed on the horizon—the *Discovery*, the *Godspeed*, and the *Susan Constant*.

For months, English men had been sailing the Atlantic Ocean toward her forest. What did they want? To make money. Investors in England were paying them to succeed in a place where many others had failed.

The men were exhausted, sick, smelly, and crabby. But the river path welcomed them safely sixty miles in from the Atlantic. They dropped anchor and called the place James Town, in honor of their ruler, King James I. Surely, just ahead were mountains of gold, the passage to China, a paradise.

Actually, just ahead was the Powhatan world.

As for the English—within months, half of these 108 men would be dead.

The mysterious new arrivals became the only topic of Powhatan conversation, but Pocahontas had no contact with them at first.

The English assumed the "naturals" would be grateful for new neighbors. Instead, the Powhatan attacked almost immediately. Outnumbering them by 140 to one, the Indians found the arrivals almost comical. They envied guns and certain metal tools, but otherwise the English way of life looked insane.

True, none of the settlers knew much about the land, like how to find roots and berries, or even fresh water. Instead they drank from the river, slimy as summer set in. This jungle was, to those who didn't know it well, an unhealthy swamp.

One by one, the men began to die.

The English leaders grew frantic, quarreling. Among them was Captain John Smith. He was a fierce soldier, age twenty-seven, always out exploring. But he wasn't as wellborn as some others, and they resented him and his ambitious ideas.

The summer sizzled on. Thick clouds of mosquitoes buzzed, carrying deadly diseases. By September, with rats and worms the only food, the English colony was about to vanish from history.

John Smith tried to learn Algonquian, the language of the Powhatan, so he could communicate. But one day, they ambushed him and took him to the chief.

Inside the royal lodge, Princess Pocahontas sat at one end, alert and curious. Warriors, priests, and wives lined up on benches, all of them clearly frightened of Chief Powhatan. Only Pocahontas showed no fear. Several of the men, glaring at Smith, had spears or heavy wooden clubs in their hands.

The two leaders spoke. Smith, besides wanting to escape with his life, hoped to win Powhatan as an ally. The chief asked when the English were leaving. Or, if they stayed, would they be *his* allies against enemies to the north and west?

Suddenly the chief went silent. Then he called for two big stones to be placed in front of him. Smith was brought forward and bent over. Warriors raised their clubs over his head.

Pocahontas cried out. Her braid flying, she ran down the hall toward Smith and covered his head with her arms and her own head. She seemed to be begging for his life.

The chief ordered the clubs to be put down.

In exchange for his release, Smith was to provide the chief with hatchets. The princess got her reward, too—pretty bells and beads.

What had Pocahontas just done? She may have been playing a role in some strategy or ritual. But the only eyewitness account we have is Smith's. He believed he was about to be killed and that she was too compassionate to let it happen.

The result was peace between one world and the other—for the time being.

Guides escorted Smith back to his shrinking settlement. And Pocahontas, with bodyguards, started to visit him. Only thirty-eight men were left now. They found Pocahontas playful and funny as she cartwheeled all over.

She and Smith taught each other words in their languages. He praised her "wit and spirit," her curiosity. Another colonist wrote, "Her especially he ever much respected."

The princess sprinted back and forth between her two different worlds, puffed with more pride than ever. No one else knew all she did.

Clearly she was Chief Powhatan's "delight and darling," someone he may even have been using as a spy.

But one night, she came alone to Smith's door. She warned him of an upcoming attack—by her father. The Powhatan and English continued as on-again, off-again enemies. And this was the second time Pocahontas saved Smith's life.

Smith, in turn, was the man most responsible for the colony's fate. He even became its president, though he still had many enemies. As more men arrived, he put them into work crews and drew up schedules. The settlement grew to contain 500 English, fifty houses, a food storehouse, and a church.

But his enemies kept plotting, and Smith was forced to return to England. Unfortunately, he didn't say good-bye to Pocahontas. We don't know why he didn't, but a royal princess deserves an explanation. Told that he was dead, she stopped visiting the English.

Right away, the colony started having trouble just getting from one day to the next. Then came the Starving Time, the disastrous winter of 1610, when food supplies ran out. Indians, their hostility more open now, kept the fort surrounded. The colonists ate their own shoes and starchy collars—they even ate each other. By spring, hundreds were dead. When another ship showed up, the sixty survivors crawled onboard, ready to sail back to England. This would have been a total victory for the Powhatan.

Except that the English moved back a day later—having encountered yet another ship with fresh supplies. So the colony limped on. Now the English, with a new leader, Captain Samuel Argall, began taking Powhatan land by force.

Another new arrival was twenty-six-year-old John Rolfe, a devoutly religious farmer intent on experimenting with *Nicotiana tabacum*: tobacco.

For four years after Smith left, Pocahontas was too busy being a princess to have anything to do with the English.

But the English never forgot her high status. In 1613, Captain Argall kidnapped her. She was about seventeen and more serious now.

In exchange for her freedom, Argall believed her fond father would do anything—give up all prisoners and runaways, weapons and tools, and much corn. Alas, nine months passed. The chief asked that she be treated with respect, but he didn't try to rescue her. He was choosing to call Argall's bluff.

Pocahontas was furious at her father's betrayal. The English described her as "exceeding pensive and discontented" at losing her freedom. But everyone agreed that her dignity never wavered. In fact, curious about all their customs, she seemed to adjust. The English coaxed her into tight dresses and shoes. They showed her how to stop sprinting and take smaller steps. Several men, among them gentle John Rolfe, taught her about their religion. The princess became the first American convert to Christianity.

Pocahontas even fell in love—with John Rolfe. Their wedding took place in James Town. Her father sent gifts and a promise for peace. The two worlds, English and Powhatan, celebrated with days of feasting, games, and her favorite thing—dancing.

A new truce began, called the Pocahontas Peace in her honor. It was a fragile one, but it allowed the colony to gain some stability.

Pocahontas had a baby, a son named Thomas. Rolfe had success with his experiment: it was tobacco, not gold, that was going to make the English investors rich.

There came another breezy day in May, this time in 1616.

Needing no help, alive with curiosity, Pocahontas climbed aboard a ship, ready to set sail with her husband and son for England. The colonists were desperate to send their elegant twenty-one-year-old princess as an ambassador. She was a way to show the investors that America was safe.

After a trip full of hardships, she crossed over London Bridge. She must have been shocked at the heads of enemies and criminals mounted on poles. And so many noisy human beings, all smashed together, hustling for money on narrow, filthy streets—most of them coughing, their lungs aflame from the burning coal in the air.

Captain John Smith begged Queen Anne to treat his old friend well. Presented at court, the princess was honored as a "natural" who could be civilized, surely the first of many. But sometimes people simply stared at her, unable to say a word. To them she was truly an alien from another world.

These English could be so ill-mannered. King James himself was flabby, grimy, and rude, especially to women— even to fellow royalty. He was exactly the opposite of the warriors Pocahontas had been brought up to respect.

Smith came to see her only once. He wrote later that they argued and that she said, "Your countrymen will lie much."

After nine months, Pocahontas liked England and wanted to stay. Why not? Her nights were devoted to dancing, her days to picnics, river walks, and games.

But Rolfe had to get back to his tobacco planting. It was her duty to follow, along with baby Thomas.

Then, with no warning, she fell ill, possibly with a fatal lung infection. Her last words to Rolfe were to comfort him: "All must die. 'Tis enough that the child lives." She may not have realized that Thomas, the first child of the old and new worlds, had also fallen sick.

She remained dignified to the end of her twenty-two years.

Back in America, the fragile peace held, but for only another year, as long as Pocahontas's father lived.

The struggling colony would continue to have ups and downs. But we know it now as Jamestown—the first English settlement in America. John Smith wrote that Pocahontas had been "the instrument to preserve this colony from death, famine, and utter confusion."

The English, thanks to a young Indian princess, had gotten what they wanted.

# STORYTELLER'S NOTE, or What Happened Next?

All the information we have on Pocahontas is from English sources—we have nothing from her perspective. Dramatic accounts of her role are often inaccurate. The 1995 Walt Disney movie, for example, is a blend of Hollywood entertainment with Shakespeare's *Romeo and Juliet*.

What we know for sure: she was born around 1595 near present-day Jamestown, Virginia; she was of high status in the Powhatan Nation; she married John Rolfe and had a son; she died in 1617, in Gravesend, Kent, England. In this book I have tried to make sense of the known facts, with the aid of the material in the Sources section, especially the books by David Price and Helen Rountree.

Two years after Pocahontas died, the Jamestown church hosted a new General Assembly—it was the birth of democracy in America. Soon there were 1,200 colonists on some forty plantations up and down the James River. The English became more aggressive toward the Indians. By 1634 the General Assembly was able to declare that the Powhatan were "no longer a nation"—they had started to disappear. Survivors fled north to Pennsylvania, New Jersey, and Canada. The last Powhatan leader was captured and killed in 1646.

Three years after Pocahontas's death, a group of English Puritans sailed on the *Mayflower* to found Plymouth Colony. Captain Smith desperately wanted to lead them, but they chose Miles Standish instead. Until Smith died in 1631, he devoted himself to promoting America as a place offering liberty, especially to poor people with ambition.

John Rolfe returned to America without his son, Thomas, who survived. Thomas never saw his father again, but he later moved to Virginia. Many in the leading families of Virginia claimed to be descendants of Pocahontas's son.

After a fire, Jamestown, the first capital of Virginia, eventually turned back into swampland. But by then Williamsburg was thriving—seven miles away—and it became the new capital in 1699.

Today, Jamestown is an archaeological site. Nearby Jamestown Settlement is a living history museum. And the Powhatan Indians did not disappear. Estimates of the population range from 13,000 to more than a million.

# SOURCES

(* especially for young readers)

Allen, Paula Gunn. *Pocahontas: Medicine Woman, Spy, Entrepreneur, Diplomat.* HarperSanFrancisco, 2003.

* Bruchac, Joseph. *Pocahontas.* Orlando: Harcourt, 2003.

* Edwards, Judith. *Jamestown, John Smith, and Pocahontas in American History.* Berkeley Heights, NJ: Enslow, 2002.

* Fritz, Jean. *The Double Life of Pocahontas.* New York: Putnam, 1983.

Historic Jamestowne, http://www.historicjamestowne.org

* Hoose, Phillip. *We Were There, Too!: Young People in U.S. History.* New York: Farrar, Straus and Giroux, 2001.

Jamestown 2007, http://www.jamestown2007.org

Jamestown Rediscovery Project, Association for the Preservation of Virginia Antiquities, http://www.apva.org/jr.html

* Jamestown Settlement and Yorktown Victory Center: A Living Museum, http://www.historyisfun.org/

Powhatan Renape Nation, http://www.powhatan.org

Price, David A. *Love and Hate in Jamestown: John Smith, Pocahontas, and the Heart of a New Nation.* New York: Knopf, 2003.

Rountree, Helen C. *Pocahontas's People: The Powhatan Indians of Virginia Through Four Centuries.* Norman: University of Oklahoma Press, 1990.

Rountree, Helen C. and E. Randolph Turner III. *Before and After Jamestown: Virginia's Powhatans and Their Predecessor.* Gainesville, FL: University Press of Florida, 2002.

Virtual Jamestown, http://www.virtualjamestown.org

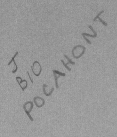

TO EMILY EASTON
–K. K.


FOR PEACHES
–D. D.

Text copyright © 2007 by Kathleen Krull
Illustrations copyright © 2007 by David Diaz

First published in the United States of America in 2007 by
Walker Publishing Company, Inc.
Distributed to the trade by Holtzbrinck Publishers

For information about permission to reproduce selections from
this book, write to Permissions, Walker & Company,
104 Fifth Avenue, New York, New York 10011

Library of Congress Cataloging-in-Publication Data
Krull, Kathleen.
Pocahontas : princess of the New World / by Kathleen Krull ; illustrations by David Diaz.
p.     cm.
ISBN-13: 978-0-8027-9554-0  •  ISBN-10: 0-8027-9554-4 (hardcover)
ISBN-13: 978-0-8027-9555-7  •  ISBN-10: 0-8027-9555-2 (reinforced)
1. Pocahontas, d. 1617—Juvenile literature. 2. Powhatan women—Biography—Juvenile literature.
3. Smith, John, 1580–1631—Juvenile literature. 4. Rolfe, John, 1585–1622—Juvenile literature.
5. Virginia—History—Colonial period, ca. 1600–1775—Juvenile literature. I. Diaz, David. II. Title.
E99.P85P63 2007        975.5'01902—dc22        [B]        2006025723

The pictures for this book were created by cutting shapes with an X-acto knife onto Rubylith.
The shapes were then scanned, arranged, and colored using Adobe Illustrator and Photoshop.

Book design by Donna Mark

Visit Walker & Company's Web site at www.walkeryoungreaders.com

First U.S. Edition 2007
Printed in the U.S.A. by Worzalla
2   4   6   8   10   9   7   5   3   1 (hardcover)
2   4   6   8   10   9   7   5   3   1 (reinforced)